John Wesley
And
Premillennialism

by

Nathaniel West

First Fruits Press
Wilmore,
Kentucky
c2018

John Wesley and premillennialism.
By Nathaniel West.
First Fruits Press, © 2018

Digital version at
http://place.asburyseminary.edu/firstfruitsheritagematerial/152/

ISBN: 9781621717768 (paperback), 9781621717775 (digital), 9781621717782 (eBook)

For all other uses, contact:

First Fruits Press
B.L. Fisher Library
Asbury Theological Seminary
204 N. Lexington Ave.
Wilmore, KY 40390
http://place.asburyseminary.edu/firstfruits

West, Nathaniel, 1826-1906.
   John Wesley and premillennialism / Nathaniel West. – Wilmore, KY : First Fruits Press, ©2018.
      55 pages ; 0.4 cm.
      Reprint. Previously published: Brooklyn, N.Y. : John de Witt, ©1894.
      ISBN: 9781621717768 (paperback)

      1. Wesley, John, 1703-1791. 2. Millennialism. I. Title.

BX8495.W5 W47 2018   287.09

Cover design by Jon Ramsay

asburyseminary.edu
800.2ASBURY
204 North Lexington Avenue
Wilmore, Kentucky 40390

First Fruits
THE ACADEMIC OPEN PRESS OF ASBURY SEMINARY

First Fruits Press
The Academic Open Press of Asbury Theological Seminary
204 N. Lexington Ave., Wilmore, KY 40390
859-858-2236
first.fruits@asburyseminary.edu
asbury.to/firstfruits

JOHN WESLEY

AND

Premillennialism

———————◆———————

" Your book on the Millennium was lately put into my hands. I cannot but thank you for your strong and seasonable confirmation of that comfortable doctrine, of which I cannot entertain the least doubt as long as I believe the Bible."—*Wesley to Rev. Thomas Hartley, M.A., Rector of Winwick, in Northamptonshire. Methodist Magazine, 1783, p. 499*

"To say that the FATHERS of the Second and Third Centuries believe the Millennial Creed of JUSTIN MARTYR, is neither more nor less than to say, they believe THE BIBLE."—*Wesley to Dr. Conyers Middleton, 1749. Wesley's Works, Vol. X, pp. 29 and 30*

Nathaniel West

———————◆◆———————

PENTECOSTAL PUB. CO.,
Louisville, Ky.

EPITAPH

To the Memory of

The Venerable John Wesley, A.M.,

Late Fellow of Lincoln College, Oxford.

This Great Light arose (by the singular providence of God) to
Enlighten these Nations, and to

REVIVE, ENFORCE, AND DEFEND THE PURE APOSTOLIC DOCTRINES AND PRACTICES

OF THE

PRIMITIVE CHURCH,

which he continued to do by his writings and his labors for
more than half a century. * * * and lived to see provision made. by the singular grace of God, for their

CONTINUANCE AND ESTABLISHMENT,

TO THE

Joy of Future Generations.

READER!

if thou art constrained to bless the instrument,

GIVE GOD THE GLORY!

In the name of God.

Amen!

A WORD OF EXPLANATION.

This excellent tract, first published something more than ten years ago, on account of the death of the author, fell out of print and circulation, and has been read by but few people. Recently Rev. L. Milton Williams, an evangelist of wide reputation, both in this land and over the ocean, found this tract, after much pains located the plates, and, after diligent search located the owner of the copyright, which he bought; and he now proposes to send the book broadcast on its heaven-born mission. The pre-millennial view of Christ's second coming is evidently in harmony with the plain teachings of the word of God. It was so understood and proclaimed by the apostles, the early Christians, and the fathers and founders of Methodism. It is quite natural that the revival of holiness should also revive an interest in the glorious hope of the appearing of our Lord. Let every reader of this tract make haste to put on the white robe, and, by the grace of God, keep themselves unspotted from the world, "for in such an hour as ye think not *the Son of Man cometh*."

H. C. MORRISON.

PREFACE.

THE history of this little tract is soon told. It was written while a guest at his home, in answer to a request of my dear friend, Mr. Harlow B. Andrews, an influential member of the University Avenue Methodist Episcopal Church, Syracuse, N. Y.; a "Barnabas, full of the Holy Ghost and of faith," and by whose labors "much people was added to the Lord." The statement, somewhat new to the ear, that "Wesley and the Oxford Methodists were lovers of the premillennial doctrine," furnished the occasion for the request. It was my pleasure to become acquainted with Professor W. P. Coddington, D.D., of Syracuse University, and desirous of submitting the manuscript to his critical revision—having all confidence in his scholarship, piety, judgment, and integrity—I did so, soliciting suggestions and corrections such as his impartial review might dictate. These, faithfully made, were as faithfully executed, and the manuscript laid aside to await the providence of God. Informed of its existence, my friend, Dr. Henry Foster, of Clifton Springs, N. Y., and others who had heard of it, expressed the wish that I would consent to allow it to see the light, with the hope that it might do something to correct a misapprehension, on the part of not a few, as to Mr. Wesley's position in reference to the Second Coming of Christ and the Millennial Age, and besides contribute to confirm the faith of many who loved the memory of Wesley, and themselves believed in what, to him, was so precious a truth.   Hearing of the manuscript, my friend, Mr. John de Witt, of Brooklyn, N. Y., solicited the perusal of it, then wrote informing me that, should I consent, it would be published at once, others concurring in the same communication.   I consented.   Dr. Coddington and others have kindly permitted their commendations to go along with it.   It is now given to the public for the glory of Christ, with the earnest prayer that this precious faith of the Wesleys, Fletcher, Coke, and the early Methodists may once more be revived as in " the olden time," and the " *hope* " that thrilled the founders of one of the greatest denominations on earth be kindled again to an undying flame.

NATHANIEL WEST.

Syracuse, July 4, 1894.

TESTIMONIALS.

From Prof. W. P. Coddington, D.D.

SYRACUSE, N. Y., *July* 3, 1893.

MY DEAR DOCTOR WEST :

Your paper on Wesley's views as to the Millennial Reign has been to me very interesting, and I may also say very instructive. I heartily hope, for the truth's sake, and for the Church's sake, you will allow its publication. It will prove a revelation to many a follower of Wesley. I have obeyed your very kind invitation for suggestions and criticism. After reading the paper several times, I find nothing therein but hard historic facts not to be gainsaid. The body of the argument, as to Wesley's position, is unanswerable, and its reassertion, in our day, seems to me very seasonable. Some words of explanation might be added as to the terms " Future Age " and " Age to Come " in the quotations from Justin and Clement of Rome, and the phrase the " Kingdom of God." I have added references to Wesley's sermon at Bradford, May, 1788, in which he refers to Bengel's view of the beginning of the Millennial Reign, and distinctly disavows any faith in his chronological calculations (*see Tyerman III, sub voce Millennium*), also to Wesley's sermons on " The Great Assize," the " New Creation," the " General Spread of the Gospel," the " General Deliverance," in which, in some places, he seems to be ambiguous. Fletcher, as the great doctrinal lawgiver and controversialist to the early Methodists, was so clear and so strong on this subject that quotations might be made from his writings. A few references to, or quotations from, John and Charles Wesley's Millennial Hymns would be very appropriate. And now, my dear brother, with you I repeat *"Amen and Amen"* to the catholic words of

Wesley, with which you close your article. We have here but a few days. God help us to stand for the truth. Names are nothing—I have often thought *worse* than nothing! Soon, how soon the Father only knows, will be the end of all things earthly; and then, through riches of infinite grace in Christ Jesus, we shall bathe in the sunlight of divine glory. O, the bliss of that *Euthanasia!* eternal communion with God, with Jesus, and the good of all ages, face to face! I am very thankful to have met you, dear brother, on this side, and to have shaken hands with you as a fellow-worker, and I know that our common prayer is, "*Lord Jesus, come! Come quickly!*" May the blissful consciousness of the Master's presence and approval be with you day by day, is the sincere prayer of your brother in the common faith and hope,

W. P. CODDINGTON.

From Prof. Ernst F. Stroeter.

UNIVERSITY PARK, COLO., *June* 9, 1894.

MY DEAR DOCTOR WEST:

I thank you, most heartily, for the privilege of reading the proof sheets of your Tract on Wesley and Premillennialism. Though it cannot make the truth of God any truer, it will prove a great help to many of Wesley's followers to see how the founders of Methodism were in the true apostolic succession of a healthy Scriptural Chiliasm. My prayer to God is that the great Methodist connection may be led by all, to whom His grace blesses the reading of your Tract, to study more closely the sure word of prophecy, and take heed to its light, as to a lamp shining in a dark place, till the Day dawn and the Day Star arise in their hearts. Perilous times are here. May the Methodist Church hold fast to, and be comforted by, the Blessed Hope of the Gospel, the Hope of the early Church, the Hope of the Fathers!

Cordially yours "in Him,"

ERNST F. STROETER.

From Rev. William Nast, D.D.

LAKESIDE, O., *June* 16, 1894.

DEARLY BELOVED DOCTOR WEST:

I bless God for the enjoyment I have experienced in reading the proof sheets you have sent me. Praise the Lord! Ever since it pleased God to reveal His Son in my heart, through the instrumentality of the Methodist Church, I have studied Wesley's writings with great diligence ; and my prayer has been that the clergy and laity of the Church might be reminded that John Wesley was a firm believer in the personal and premillennial coming of the Lord Jesus, not for the closing judgment in His administration, but to usher in a blessed millennial age, during which the Nations will be under His personal reign as the Only Potentate, and Prince of the Kings of the earth, even as the best believers, now, are under the sway of His grace. And, now, bless God! my prayer has been answered in a way I did not expect! My heart overflows! O, for the day when, body and soul, we shall be "like Him," the blessed Lord, to all eternity!

Forever yours in the Hope of His Coming and His Kingdom,

WILLIAM NAST.

From Henry Foster, M.D.

CLIFTON SPRINGS, N. Y., *June* 10, 1894.

MY DEAR BROTHER WEST :

I have just finished reading the advanced sheets of your Tract on Wesley and Premillennialism, and thank God that you have collected so many facts respecting Wesley's faith on the subject of the Coming of the Lord, and its relation to the future Age. I do hope that your labor may be greatly blessed of the Lord, for it throws a flood of light on the whole subject and shows the faith and force of the early Church, and also of the Wesleyan revival. This Blessed Hope has inspired my life for more than forty years, and I believe that the publication of your Tract will do much toward bringing our Church again to its original zeal and power in the great work of doing and suffering for Christ, and preparing the way for His glorious coming.

Ever yours in Christ,

HENRY FOSTER.

From H. B. Andrews.

NORTH ADAMS, MASS., *May* 25, 1894.

DEARLY BELOVED BROTHER:

I learn, with great gratitude to God, that your manuscript on Wesley and Premillennialism is to appear in print. Reared, from my youth, in the Methodist Church which I love, my father himself a Methodist minister, my education, like his had led me to believe that John Wesley taught the post-millennial view of the Coming of our Lord. My reading of Wesley's own writings, however, and especially of your manuscript, has convinced me that while he believed in the universal spread of the Gospel, and the power of Revivals, he as fully believed there could be no millennium till the Lord comes, and that the Coming of the Lord is the " Hope " of the Church. He certainly held the faith of the primitive Church. Your Tract will enlighten many. Bless God! May it serve to rekindle the old fires again, and be the means of awakening the prayer throughout our whole denomination, " *Lord Jesus, come quickly !* " We need His bright Appearing and His Kingdom.

In His Name, ever yours,

H. B. ANDREWS

JOHN WESLEY ON PREMILLENNIALISM.

THE full text of Wesley's word to Dr. Middleton, partly
on the title-page of this tract, is the following: "The
doctrine (as you well know) which *Justin* deduced from
the Prophets and Apostles, and in which he was undoubtedly followed by the Fathers of the second and third centuries, is this. *The souls of them who have been martyred*
for the witness of Jesus, and for the word of God, and of
those who have not worshiped the Beast, neither received
his mark, shall live and reign with Christ a Thousand
Years. But the rest of the dead shall not live again until
the Thousand Years are finished. Now, to say they [the
Fathers] believe this, *is neither more nor less than to say,*
THEY BELIEVE THE BIBLE." *

The force of Wesley's words to the Rev. Mr. Hartley
will be considered later on. Meanwhile, it is proper to say
of *Justin* that he was of Roman descent, and born of
heathen parents, in Palestine, shortly before or after the
death of the Apostle John. He received a high education in
all the great schools of philosophy, was first a Stoic, then
a Platonist, last of all, a convert to Christianity, still wear-
ing the cloak of the philosopher. He became one of the
most learned and eloquent defenders of the Christian Faith

* *Wesley's Works, Emory's edition, V,* 726, 727.

in the second century. He was profoundly versed in the Scriptures. At Ephesus he disputed with Trypho the Jew, at Rome with Crescens the Gentile, and everywhere in the cities of Europe and Asia stood forth as the champion of the truth and of the suffering Church. He addressed his first "*Apology*" for the Christian Religion to the Emperor Antoninus Pius; his second, to the Roman Senate. His martyrdom is variously assigned to A. D. 161–168, as his birth has been to A. D. 89–113. His influence was unlimited, and his name is a sacred heirloom throughout the Christian world. It is of this man's faith Wesley speaks. Whoever knows John Wesley's character as a scholar, or debater, or man of cautious language and positive convictions, will be able to appreciate his estimate of the premillennial creed of the early Church, and her hope of the Coming of the Lord. That doctrines dear to Wesley's heart, preached, advocated, and defended by him, built upon the word of God, and attested by the martyrs, should be thrown into the background, or denied, or opposed by Christian men, is one of the astounding developments in the so-called progress of the Christian Church. Over his grave words were written that can never be forgotten. His epitaph says he was raised up of God to "*Revive, Enforce, and Defend the Pure Apostolic Doctrines and Practices of the Primitive Church*,"—did so for "*more than Half a Century*,"—and "*lived to see provision made for their Continuance and Establishment, to the joy of future generations.*" Nothing can be stronger than this. Was Wesley wrong in holding the Premillennial Faith, or believing so earnestly in the Second Coming of the Lord? Are his statements wrong in reference to Justin's Creed, and the faith of the Church of the second and third centuries? Is his epitaph untrue? On the contrary, all is true, and the purpose of this brief writing is to show *how* true was all that Wesley said in reference to this subject.

I.—JUSTIN MARTYR'S CREED.

It is found particularly given in his celebrated "*Dialogue*" with Trypho the Jew, held at Ephesus. The Jew asks, "*Do you confess that this place, Jerusalem, shall be rebuilt, and your people be congregated, and rejoice together with Christ and the Patriarchs and Prophets?*"

The answer of Justin is:

"*I confessed to you, before, that I and many others, besides, do believe, as you well know, this shall be. On the other hand, I have also signified to you that* MANY, WHO ARE NOT OF THE PURE AND PIOUS FAITH OF THE CHRISTIANS, DO NOT CONFESS THIS.* *They are called Christians, indeed, but are godless impious* HERETICS, *because they teach doctrines that, in every respect, are blasphemous, atheistic, foolish. . . . They do not confess this, but dare to blaspheme the God of Abraham, Isaac, and Jacob, and say there is no resurrection of the dead, but that at death souls are received up into heaven. Do not imagine that these are Christians.* But I and others, who are orthodox on all points, know there will be a Resurrection from the dead and a Thousand Years in Jerusalem, built again, broadened, and adorned, as the prophets Ezekiel, Isaiah, and others declare. A certain man among us, of the name of John, one of the Apostles of Christ, in a Revelation which he had, prophesied that they who were faithful to our Messiah would accomplish a *Thousand*

---

* Justin refers to the *Gnostics*.

Years in Jerusalem, and after that the general, and to speak concisely, the final Resurrection and Judgment of all would take place" (*Dialogue with Trypho, chapters* 80, 81).

II.—CREED OF THE PRIMITIVE CHURCH.

And this creed of Justin was the creed of the whole Apostolic Church, and of the Church nearest the Apostles for three hundred years, save the " heretics," who denied it. Justin speaks, not as a private individual giving his individual opinion, but as a public person and open " witness "* to the faith of the " Primitive Church." And Wesley defends Justin and the Fathers, and says of them, that to say that they believe it "*is neither more nor less than to say that they believe* THE BIBLE." The Apostolic Fathers are divided into four schools,—the school of John, the school of Peter, the school of Paul, the school of James. Let us take a specimen from each in support of Wesley's statement.

(1.) BARNABAS said : " The true Sabbath is the Sabbath of the *Thousand Years.* Then all will be sanctified completely when we shall have become perfectly righteous,—that is, *when Christ comes back to reign.* The righteous man expects the holy age. Then, he shall rise from the dead." †

(2.) CLEMENT of Rome (Phil. 4. 3) tells us that "the Apostles, assured by the resurrection of Christ and their conversation with Him, all went forth proclaiming the good news that *the Kingdom of God would come,* the

---

* The Fathers speak as *Witnesses*, testifying what was the belief of the Church in their time (Daillé on the Use of the Fathers, 189, 288-290, *Chillingworth's Works*, 729-734).

† Donaldson, *Apost. Fath.*, 230, 240 ; Dressel, *Patr. Opp.*, 24, 43.

righteous be *manifested* in the Kingdom, and the martyrs receive their reward from Him who is the Fashioner and the Father of the ages." *

(3.) POLYCARP, the "*Angel of Smyrna*" (Rev. 2. 8) and pupil of John said : "Whoever denies the Resurrection is the *First-Born of Satan!* If we obey Christ, and please Him in this present age, *we shall receive the Age to come. He will raise us from the dead, and we shall live and reign with Him.* The saints shall judge the world " (Ibid., 183, 192 ; Ibid., 382).

(4.) HERMAS, the "*Shepherd*," the Bunyan of his time (Rom. 16. 14): "*The Elect of God will dwell in the Future Age, and remain pure and unstained.* They will all be joyful then. All things will be smooth to them, if they keep His Commandments. They shall obtain Victory and Reward, but the World that now is shall be destroyed by fire. *This Age is Winter to the just ; the Coming Age is* SUMMER " (Ibid., 305 ; Ibid., 586).

These are specimens only. A volume might be added. Was Wesley right or wrong when he said Justin's Premillennial Creed was the Creed of the second century? One of the greatest of modern scholars, Professor Dorner, of Berlin, writing about these Apostolic Fathers, says : "*All were at one ;* the men of the *Johannine* school, like Polycarp and Papias ; of the *Pauline*, like Ignatius and Clement of Rome ; of the *Petrine*, like Barnabas ; of that of *James*, like Hermas and Hegesippus " (*Person of Christ I*, 143). Dr. Schaff says : "They all shine with the evening red of the apostolic day, and breathe an enthusiasm of simple faith and fervent love, and fidelity to the Lord, which proved its power in suffering and martyrdom " (*Ch. Hist. I*, 457).

---

* Donaldson, *Apost. Fath.*, 143, 150 ; Dressel, *Patr. Opp.*, 86, 88.

III.—STILL FURTHER CONFIRMED.

Let us verify Wesley's statement as to the Fathers of the third century. What was their Creed? We add:

(5.) IRENÆUS "the Great," pupil of Polycarp, says: "Christ is the Stone cut out of the mountain, without hands, *who shall destroy temporal kingdoms, and introduce an eternal one, which is at the Resurrection of the just.* When the Antichrist shall have devastated all things, and shall reign for three years and a half (1,260 days) and sit in the temple at Jerusalem, then the Lord will come from Heaven, with the clouds, in the glory of the Father, sending this man to the lake of fire, but bringing in, for the righteous, *the Times of the Kingdom, the Rest, the Hallowed Seventh Day, and restoring to Abraham the Promised Inheritance.* Christ will Himself renew the inheritance of the Earth, and reorganize the mystery of the glory of His sons. In the Times of the Kingdom *the Righteous shall bear rule when they rise from the dead,* and then Creation shall be renovated. The Earth shall be called by Christ to its pristine condition, *and Jerusalem rebuilt after the pattern of the Jerusalem which is the Mother of us all.* . . . Man rises, not allegorically, from the dead, as I have shown repeatedly. And as he rises actually, so shall he be actually disciplined beforehand for incorruption, and shall go forward and flourish in the Times of the Kingdom. *John, therefore, did distinctly foresee the* 'FIRST RESURRECTION,' *that of the just, and the Inheritance in the Kingdom on Earth"* (*Iren. Adv. Hæres. V,* 26, 30, 33, 35).

(6.) LACTANTIUS, the "Christian Cicero," and preceptor of Constantine's son: "It is ordained by the disposal of God Most High that *the present unrighteous Age,—* a space of time having been accomplished,—*shall have an end*, when, *wickedness becoming extinct, and the souls of the godly called back to a blessed life, there shall flourish a quiet, tranquil, peaceable and Golden Age, the Lord Himself then reigning.* The righteous King will institute a great Judgment on the earth respecting the living and the dead, and will deliver the Nations in subjection to the righteous who shall be alive. *He will raise the righteous dead to eternal life, and will Himself reign with them on the earth, and will build the Holy City, and this Kingdom of the righteous shall be for a Thousand Years.* Then the Last Judgment will come to pass against the Nations. Then the wicked shall arise, not to life, but to punishment. The *Second Resurrection* shall take place. *This is the doctrine of the holy prophets which we Christians follow*" (*Div. In·tt, Lib. IV, cap.* 2, *and VII, cap.* 26).

This is more than enough to justify Wesley's reply to Dr. Middleton. The creed of Justin was the creed of the purest Church that ever trod the earth, and the nearest to the Apostles. It was the creed of men who learned it from the Apostles themselves, and found it in the Prophets as well; a creed in which, as Dr. Donaldson, one of England's best scholars, says, " There is not a syllable to intimate a single enjoyment that is not consistent with the utmost holiness " (*Hist. Chr. Lit. II,* 263);—a creed which, as Neander says, though on the part of a few was sometimes mixed with " subordinate notions," was neither gross nor Jewish in a carnal sense, but "filled with an exalted idea of the blessedness of fellowship with God" (*Chh. Hist. I,* 651);—a creed which, Dr. Schaff says, was "*a precious hope*," and which Lange calls "*a pearl of true doctrine.*" Was Wesley wrong in defending it as the "*pure faith*" of the "*Primitive Church?*" Is his "*Epitaph*" a libel on his name? No! It was the creed not only of the great men already named who battled for the faith in the front line of the Christian conflict, and sealed it with martyr-blood,—but of Tertullian, Melito, Hippolytus, Cyprian, Cyril, Nepos, Commodian, Methodius, Victorinus, Gregory of Nyssa, Sulpicius, Paulinus, Athanasius,—giants of the faith, the creed of a Church that overturned the Roman Empire. *Wesley was right.* It was a creed, built on the Prophets, the great Olivet discourse of our Lord concerning the End, on the Apostolic Epistles, and in the Apocalypse given to John. It had a sure foundation.

IV.—YET MORE CONFIRMED.

But the assertion of Wesley is yet more confirmed, by a phalanx of Church historians and scholars before and since Wesley's day. "It was," says Gieseler, "the general belief of the apostolic age" (*Eccl. Hist. I,* § 166). "It was," says Mede, the ablest scholar of his day, "the general belief of all orthodox Christians in the age next following the Apostles, and none but Heretics denied it " (*Works,* 602, 771). "It was," says Hase, "the old and popular faith" (*Hist. Chh.,* 688). "The stream of all antiquity ran that way," says Holmes (*Resurr. Revealed,* 370). So Muencher: "It was universally held by almost all teachers " (*Chh. Hist. II,* 415). "It was," says the great Chillingworth, champion of the Bible and the Protestant faith, "the doctrine believed and taught by the most eminent Fathers of the Church in the age next after the Apostles, and by none of that age opposed or condemned " (*Works,* 482). Burton, of Oxford, in the Bampton Lectures for 1829, affirms that "the early Church's faith in the premillennial advent of the Lord is beyond successful denial " (*Lectures, p.* 84). So speak Bishops Russell, Newton, and Horne, the former saying, "It was the sure and certain faith entertained by the Christian world down to the beginning of the fourth century " (*Lectures,* 1839, *p.* 284). "The whole Church," says Alford, "for three hundred years held it, and it is the most cogent instance of unanimity which primitive antiquity presents " (*N. T. II, part* 2, *p.* 1088). It was the faith of the Nicene Council, A. D. 325, which quoted our Lord's "*Third Beatitude* " in its support, as Wesley does: "The meek shall inherit the earth" (*Hist. Act. Conc. Nic., Lib. II, cap.* 29). It never was abandoned until *Church and State* were united under Constantine; never until, as Kurtz says truly, "*The State-Church under her temporal prosperity forgot the millennial glory of the future* " (*Chh. Hist. I,* 47), and the Church, as the great BENGEL, whom Wesley took for his teacher, says, "became worldly, and the hope of the future was weakened by the joy over the present success!" (*Erklärt Offenbarung,* 664.) Then, and only then, did she depart from the martyr faith, under the teaching of Rome and the influence of worldly philosophy, so that, as Canon Faussett well says, "Christians began looking at the *temporal prosperity* and *ceased to look for Christ's promised reign on earth* " (*Comm. VI, Introd. to Apoc.,* 70).

V.—HARTLEY'S BOOK.

The second extract on the title page of this tract is Wesley's word to Rev. Thomas Hartley, M.A., Rector of Winwick, Northamptonshire, England. It was this: "Your book on the MILLENNIUM was lately put into my hands.

I cannot but thank you for your strong and seasonable confirmation of that comfortable doctrine, *of which I cannot
entertain the least doubt as long as I believe the Bible.*"
And what was Hartley's doctrine which Wesley so strongly
commended, and fully believed ?   The standard three-vol-
umed edition of the *"Life and Times of Rev. John Wesley,
M.A., Founder of the Methodists, by the Rev. L. Tyerman,
Harper Brothers, New York,* 1872," provides us with
authentic information in reference to this important work
and its author.   Of Mr. Hartley it says, " He was a friend
of the Countess of Huntingdon and of the Shirley family ;
a man of learning and of strong cultivated mind.   He was
an earnest, devout, energetic Christian, an able, liberal,
unbigoted   minister,"   etc., etc.   Of Mr. Hartley's book,
" *Paradise Restored*" (p. 356, 8vo), Mr. Tyerman says,
" It is, by far, the most sober, sensible, scriptural, and
learned work on the Millennium that it has been our lot to
read.   He professes to show 'the great importance of the
doctrine of Christ's glorious reign on earth with his saints,'
and maintains that 'it was typified in many of the Levitical
Institutes ; was foretold and described in numberless places
by the inspired prophets; was made the subject of many
precious promises in the Gospel ; was delineated in the
Revelation of St. John ; and was received as an apostolical
doctrine by the primitive Christians, according to the testimony of the ancient fathers, as Barnabas, Hermas, Justin
Martyr, Irenæus, Tertullian, and Lactantius.'   He further
argues that it received the sanction of the Council of Nice
called by Constantine the Great, and composed of Bishops
from all parts of the Christian world ; and that it is embodied
in the Catechism of King Edward VI, which was revised by
the English Bishops, and published by royal authority in

the last year of King Edward's reign." * Limited space makes possible only some of the *Chief Points* of Mr. Hartley's book. And these are: "(1) That Christ will come a second time, and will set up a kingdom, and visibly reign on the earth for a thousand years. (2) That, during this reign His saints will be raised, and restored to the perfection of the first man Adam ; and earth all over will become a copy of the Primæval Paradise. (3) That, during this millennial theocracy, saints will flourish, and sinners will be in absolute subjection ; hostility and discord will cease, and all things harmonize in unity and peace. (4) That some of the saints will be crowned, some sit on thrones, set over ten cities, or five, some sit at the table with Christ, and others serve; some follow the Lamb whithersoever he goes; others come periodically to worship in his presence." On some of these points, as on others, Mr. Hartley does not positively decide, as for instance: "(1) The duration of this holy empire. (2) Whether its administration will be under the constant abiding presence of our Lord's visible humanity, or only occasional manifestations of it. (3) Whether the universal conflagration will be before or after the millennial reign. (4) Whether the subjects of this kingdom will consist only of the saints who are living at the time of Christ's advent, and of some others, as martyrs who will be raised from the dead, or whether there will be a continued succession of the redeemed ones raised, according to their order and time," etc. "These," says Mr. Tyerman, " are some of the salient points of Mr. Hartley's learned and able book. Why are they enumerated here ? Because, in substance, they were held by Mr. Wesley. Wesley read the book, and read it with approbation. He writes to the

* *Tyerman's Life and Times, etc., II,* 521-524.

author, ' Your book on the *Millennium* was lately put into
my hands. I cannot but thank you for your strong and
seasonable confirmation of that comfortable doctrine, of
which *I cannot entertain the least doubt as long as I believe the Bible.*' With such a statement, in reference to
such a book, there can be no doubt that Wesley, *like his
father before him*, was a *Millenarian*, a believer in the
second advent of Christ to reign on earth, visibly and glor-
iously, for a thousand years."* So much for the book of
Hartley.

VI.–FREEDOM FROM VAGARIES.

If ever anyone was free from the " vagaries " and " whim-
sies " of certain premillennialists who substituted their own
notions for the word of God, it was Wesley. He believed
a great work of missions to the heathen had yet to be done
before the coming of the Lord, that Israel also must be
prepared to welcome Him, and that the Antichrist precedes
the Advent. Especially did he repel all attempts to fix a
date for the Advent. On this point he wrote specially to
Mr. Thomas Carill, saying, " I have no opinion at all upon
when the millennial reign of Christ will begin [*i. e.*, as to
any *date*]. I can determine nothing at all about it. These
calculations are far above, out of my sight." † And again,
in " Letters to a Young Disciple," he says, " I do not determine any of these things. They are too high for me."‡
He owed much to the great Bengel, but fortunately avoided
what were Bengel's two mistakes, viz.: (1) That of a
"*Double Millennium*," a mistake due to a supposed

---

* *Life and Times, etc., by Tyerman, II*, 522, 523.
† *Ibid.*, 524.
‡ *Wesley's Works, Emory's edition, VII*, 730.

necessity for the definite article in Revelation 20. 2, 4, 6; and
(2) that of endeavoring to *fix a date* for the Advent.   In all
else, Bengel was his guide in prophecy.   For a time, the
prevalence of the *Whitbyan Theory*, or " *New Hypothe-
sis*,"—even yet so common among the spiritualizers of
prophecy, caused him to interpret the " *leaven* " in the
parable as meaning the sanctifying grace of God.   Still he
held firmly, with all the early Fathers, the Reformers, the
English Church to which he belonged, and with the triumphant school of exegesis inaugurated by Bengel,—even
as all standard exegetes now hold,—that there will be *no
universal conversion of the world* before the Lord comes,
but that the world will end in a Judgment of the living
wicked and of false Christianity, as it will in the Redemp-
tion of the righteous.   It was the common doctrine of
Justin, Irenæus, and Tertullian ; of Luther, Calvin, and
Knox ; of Cranmer, Latimer, and Ridley ; of Bengel, the
Moravians, the Pietists, and of English Churchmen and
Dissentists.   It is what the great body of evangelical
believers hold to-day all over Christendom.

It is therefore an error to suppose that Wesley was inconsistent with himself.   A transient ambiguity of expression
in a theme of such wide relations is insufficient to justify
such a conclusion.   It is true he interpreted the parable
of the *leaven* as the spread of the Gospel.   In replying to
the charge that *the world will never become Christian*,
and Christianity must fail, he makes three special answers
in his Sermon on " *The General Spread of the Gospel*,"
viz. : (1) the supposition of " irresistible grace " on all mankind, a " possible," but " not probable," solution ; (2) the
supposition of " the general and gradual spread of the
Gospel," a " highly probable " solution, and a popular one

in his day, when a revival fifty years long was so mighty, and the Whitby theory was in vogue. Yet he does not dogmatize, but (3) he is *sure* there will be no conversion of the world before Israel, the Jews as a people, are literally restored to their land and converted to Christ, which prophecy puts in connection with the Lord's coming, *i. e.*, when Acts 3. 19–21, Rom. 11. 25, 26, Isa. chapter 11, Jer. 33, and Ezek. 36 : 37, are literally fulfilled. "*At that time the work will be done.*" " *This is the only full satisfactory answer that can be given*" (*Sermons II*, 74–82. *Hunt & Eaton, N. Y.*). He thoroughly believed in a full development, also of the Great Apostasy in the very heart of Christendom. (*II*, 64, 65.) In his Sermon on "*The General Deliverance*," he holds that "the whole creation" will "groan in pain" until the Lord comes. (*II*, 49–57.) The Third Beatitude belongs to the Millennial Age, after the First Resurrection. (*I*, 191.) All the great missionary movements, the revivals occurring, and the judicial blinding of unbelievers, with the worldliness of the clergy, and increase of corruption by means of wealth, are "*Signs*" of the approaching end. (*II*, 93.) In chronological computations he had no faith. (*Tyerman II*, 524.)

Two years before he had completed the final enlarged edition of his " *Notes on the New Testament* " guided by Bengel, he preached his sermon on the "*Great Assize*," 1758, at Bradford. In this sermon he presents the *whole end* in one undiscriminated picture, after the manner of the earlier prophets, and followed their law of perspective representation : two Ends in one End, two Resurrections in one Resurrection,—two Judgments in one universal and simultaneous Judgment of all mankind, living and dead, while yet they are separate. He blends all the Scripture texts concerning the End of our present age, and of the Millennial Age, in one scene. By this means the "Thousand Years" are thrown into Eternity, the two Ends being thus brought close together, for the sake of practical effect, as one scene, in the same general discourse concerning the final destinies of men. He is not hereby inconsistent with his exegesis which, elsewhere, separates these ages and ends. Like the Earlier Prophets, he sees the Millennial and Eternal ages in one. Like the later revelation in Daniel, Ezekiel, and John, he also sees them apart. It is the manner of prophecy thus to view the Total End in one picture, a crowning example of which we have in our Lord's Olivet Discourse. What homiletically, pictorially, and practically appears as *one*, is exegetically and critically *two*. We misunderstand Wesley, if we think that, by the one representation, he denies the other. (*I*, 126.)

VII.—ADDITIONAL INFORMATION.

Wesley taught, specifically : (1) The spread of the Gospel as a testimony to all nations; (2) an Apostasy yet more to be developed, and already at work, in Christendom ; (3) the literal Conversion and Restoration of Israel to their own land ; (4) that the full revelation of the Antichrist precedes the Advent ; (5) that it is the duty of the Church to observe the Signs of the Times ; (6) the literal, visible, personal, and glorious Second Coming of the Lord ; (7) that the Third Beatitude, "the meek shall inherit the earth," refers to the Millennial Age, (8) that the curse shall be removed from the earth, and the animal creation restored to pristine innocence; (9) that there shall be a transfiguration of the Planet into a New Earth, with a New Heaven, and a New Climate ; (10) that it is the duty of the Church, always, to pray and look for the Coming of the Lord.*

How else could it be ? The Word of God is clear enough, and Wesley's whole training could produce no other result. His father was a premillennialist. The English Church to which they both belonged was such from the days of the Great Reformation.   All the early Oxford Methodists were the same, and tenacious, not only of the "Articles of Faith," but of "King Edward's Catechism," composed by Cranmer and premillennial to the core. The Moravians of Fetter Lane, in London, whom Wesley joined, were premillennialists, as were the Moravians and Pietists in Germany whom Wesley visited and where he found "*a heaven to his soul.*" The "Orphan House of Francke" was "*full of blessing.*" He was personally acquainted with Zinzendorf, and that missionary miracle of grace, David.   The two men who were the means of Wesley's conversion, after his fourteen years of legalism, were Peter Bohler, ordained by Zinzendorf, and Martin Luther, whose "Preface to the Romans " was blessed to the full salvation of his soul—both premillennialists.   Spangenberg, a devout Moravian, was his bosom friend. His brother, Charles Wesley, was the premillennial poet of the Church, and, like so many other sacred poets of the time, sang in thrilling numbers, the Coming King. The immortal Fletcher, dear to his heart, was one of the most rapturous and thoroughgoing premillennialists ever known. So was Wesley's friend, the Vicar of Bexley.† Bengel, his great teacher and guide,

---

* *Sermons. Emory's edition, Hunt & Eaton, New York. I*, 191 ; *II*, 54, 55, 65, 81, 86, 87. 94, 95, 98 ; and *Notes on Rev., cap*. XIX, XXII.

† *Life and Times, by Tyerman, I*, 67, 69, 73, 179, 180. *Tyerman's Fletcher*, 20, 21, 376, 377, 536-538.

was " the father of modern premillennialism." Think of it ! Luther, Bengel, Francke, Zinzendorf, Bohler, Spangenberg, and David,—the early Fathers,—the memories of Cranmer, Latimer, and Ridley,—all going to make up Wesley! How else could he speak of Justin's creed? How else of Hartley's book?

VIII.—JOHN ALBRIGHT BENGEL.

Such the name of Wesley's great guide in exegesis and prophecy, and without whom we had never seen Wesley's "*Notes on the New Testament,*" and especially upon the "*Apocalypse.*" There is not a university in the world where Bengel's works and name are not held in the highest honor. The greatest of scholars have knelt at his shrine. He led the whole Christian Church in the exposition of the Sacred Scriptures. To be praised by the great will be his lot while time lasts. " To whom do we owe it," asks Delitzsch, "that *the orthodox Church of the present time no longer brands premillennialism as a heresy, so that there is scarcely a believing Christian now who does not hold it? We owe it to Bengel.*" * It is of Bengel Professor Dorner says, "His works were the first cock-crowing of that new kind of exegesis the Church so much needed." † It is Luthardt who says, "Long time had the study of the prophetic word, in its true light, been unknown to the Church. In Bengel the conscience of the Church lifted a loud cry against the neglect of the Apocalypse. From Bengel, the light gleamed out over the Old Testament also, and opened up a brighter view into the Times of the earthly completion of the Church and the relation of the

---

* *Biblico-Prophetic Theol.,* 27.
† *Hist. Prot. Theol. II,* 233.

same to Israel, and began to burst the chains of the old dogmatic tradition. From Bengel went forth that deep investigation of Prophecy and its Fulfillment which extends to our own time in ever-increasing breadth and depth, and has given us our more perfect understanding of both the Old and New Testaments."* It is impossible to exaggerate the praise that is poured upon the head of Wesley's great teacher,—a man among the devoutest and most learned that ever appeared to unfold the word of God. And what said Wesley? Writing to Joseph Benson upon the merits of different interpreters of prophecy, Wesley says: "Undoubtedly Bishop Newton's book on the Prophecies is well written, and he is certainly a man of sense and understanding. This he has shown in what he writes on the Revelation. . . . But there is no comparison, either as to sense, learning, or piety, between Newton and Bengel. The former is a mere child to the latter."† Again, speaking of his inability to understand the Prophecies, he says: "I did not study them at all, for many years, and perhaps I should have lived and died in this sentiment had I not seen the works of the great BENGELIUS. But these revived my hopes of understanding even the prophecies of this book,—the Revelation. The following *Notes* are mostly those of that excellent man; a few of which are taken from his *Gnomon Novi Testamenti*, but far more from his *Erklärte Offenbarung*, which is a full and regular Comment on the Revelation."‡ And again, "I once designed to write down what barely occurred to my own mind, consulting none but the inspired writers. But no

---

* *Doctrine of the Last Things,* 28.
† *Wesley's Works, Emory's edition, Vll,* 79.
‡ *Wesley's Notes on the Revelation. Preface, p.* 650.

sooner was I acquainted with that great light, BENGELIUS, than I entirely changed my design, being thoroughly convinced that it might be of more service to the Cause of Religion were I barely to translate his *Gnomon Novi Testamenti* than to write any volumes upon it. Many of his excellent notes I have therefore translated ; many more I have abridged." * Behold the great Master and the great Pupil,—both premillennialists! *The foundations of the Methodist Church were laid deep in the premillennial faith of the pure apostolic and primitive martyr Church,* and would God but revive once more, in the hearts of her Bishops, Elders, Pastors, and Itinerating Ministry, the ancient faith that overturned the Roman Empire and kindled the souls of the two Wesleys, Fletcher, Coke, and the "Oxford Methodists," and gave to Bengel his undying fame, and yet beats in the souls of thousands of God's dear children of different denominations to-day, what a conflagration of holy fervor and vital Christianity would sweep over our now secularized churches, and over our land so enslaved to material interests and to mammon ! May the spirit of the early martyrs, to " *revive, enforce, and defend* " whose "*pure apostolic doctrines and practices* " Wesley was raised up "*by the singular providence of God*," the spirit and the creed of Polycarp, Justin, and Irenæus,—of Spener, Bengel, David, and Francke,—soon return ! May the Millennial Songs of Charles Wesley, Watts, Heber, Montgomery, and how many more of later times, resound again in every temple, and in every camp ground, to the praise of the Coming King ! What multitudes,— under the flaming tongues of our modern Evangelists, and of the Gospel and Salvation Armies, have been charmed

* *Wesley's Notes on New Testament. Preface, p. 4.*

into life eternal by these melodies! What multitudes more, everywhere, in our City Missions, in the highways and the hedges, lost among the lost, are waiting to hear again this minstrelsy from heaven! The Lord pour upon us all the inspiration that gave birth to the 72nd Psalm!

IX.—THE THOUSAND YEARS.

Wesley believed in *no Millennium before the Lord comes visibly and personally from an opened Heaven to destroy the Antichrist.* This is most certain. He makes, as did Bengel, in accord with the creed of the "*Primitive Church,*" and the Holy Scriptures, the Thousand Years FOLLOW the Lord's return. Commenting on Revelation XIX, XX, he says: "*And I saw Heaven Opened, and Behold a White Horse, and Him that sitteth on him,*" etc., etc. This is a new and peculiar opening, in order to show the Magnificent Expedition of Christ and His attendants, against His great Adversary. Many little regarded Christ when He came meek and lowly riding on an *Ass!* But what will they say when he goes forth upon His *White Horse,* with the sword of His mouth! . . . *Jesus Christ Himself overthrows the Beast!* The proud Dragon shall be bound by an angel. *That the one thousand years do not precede, nor run parallel with the Times of the Beast, but* WHOLLY FOLLOW *the Times of the Beast,* may manifestly appear (1) From the Series of the whole Book representing one continued chain of events; (2) From the circumstances which precede; (3) These 1,000 years bring a new, full, and lasting immunity from all outward and inward evils, and an affluence of all blessings. But such a time the Church has never yet seen. Therefore, it is still to come. What occurs from Chapter XX, 11, to

Chapter XXII, 5, manifestly FOLLOWS the things related in Chapter XIX. THE ONE THOUSAND YEARS COME BE-TWEEN. The fulfillment approaches nearer and nearer. We are shortly to expect the calamities, one after another, occasioned by the Second Beast, the Harvest, Vintage, the Pouring out of the Phials, the Judgment of Babylon, the last raging of the Beast and his Destruction, and the Imprisonment of Satan. There is no counsel against the Lord." *

X.—THE ADVENT.

" *The Spirit and the Bride say,* COME! The Spirit of Adoption in the Bride, and in the heart of every true believer, says with earnest desire and expectation, COME! and accomplish all the words of this prophecy! *And let him that thirsteth Come!* Here, they also that are farther off are invited. *And whosoever will, let him take the water of life freely,*—as freely as he drinks of the running stream! The Apostle adds that all the plagues shall be added to him who adds to this Book. He that takes from it, all the blessings shall be taken from him. *And, doubtless, this* GUILT *is incurred by all those who lay hindrances in the way of the faithful, which prevent them from hearing the Lord's* ' I COME,'—*and from answering,* COME, LORD JESUS! He that testifieth these things,—even all that is contained in this Book,—saith, for the encouragement of the *Church* in all her afflictions, ' YEA,'—answering the call of the Spirit and the Bride,—' I COME QUICKLY!'— to destroy all her enemies, and establish her in a state of perfect and everlasting happiness. The Apostle expresses his earnest desire and hope of this, by answering ' AMEN!

* *Notes on the Revelation, pp. 720, etc.*

COME, LORD JESUS!' The free love of the Lord Jesus and all its fruits *be with all who thus long for His Appearing!"* *

O that this last sigh and sweetest prayer of the beloved disciple might once more be breathed from the hearts, pulpits, prayerrooms, and homes not only of the Methodist, but of all denominations!—" *Come,*" the sweetest word—" *Lord Jesus,*" the sweetest Name,—in all the Gospel!

XI.—FLETCHER'S TESTIMONY.

The Rev. John William Fletcher, Vicar of Madeley, Shropshire, England, was born in Nyon, Switzerland, 1729, and died in Madeley, 1785. His name is illustrious in the annals of Methodism. The first line of his epitaph declares him to have been " a man eminent for genius, eloquence, and theological learning." He was a man of whom the poet Southey said, " No Church ever possessed a more apostolic minister," and whom Isaac Taylor called " as unearthly a being as could tread the earth at all." The great Robert Hall described him as a " seraph burning with the ardor of divine love." John Wesley esteemed him so highly as " to request him to be his successor." He was educated at the University of Geneva, and when eighteen years of age " began to study the prophecies of the Holy Bible." The companion of an aged and eminent divine who had " spent fifty years to make himself master of the Oriental languages, and to explain the various predictions of the Old and New Testaments," he became, from personal conviction, a glowing advocate of the premillennial

---

* *Notes on the Revelation, pp.* 723, 731.

faith. " Of this fact," says Mr. Tyerman, his biographer,
" there cannot be a doubt." *

Speaking of Fletcher's celebrated letter written to Wesley
Nov. 29, 1775, on the Second Coming of Christ and His
Millennial Reign, Mr. Tyerman remarks: " It is, in all
respects, a remarkable production. He expresses his belief
that the End of the world is drawing near, and adduces
elaborate reasons for this opinion. He confesses his belief
in the Second Coming of the Saviour, and in His personal
reign on earth for a thousand years. It is too long to be
inserted here. It may be read in the *Methodist Magazine
for* 1793, and is of importance as showing that the millenarian theory, now attracting so much attention, found con-
siderable favor among some of the most distinguished
of the first Methodists." †

It is in this letter, 1755, he holds that the rising tide of
infidelity, the wars, earthquakes, persecutions, and calamities
of the latter half of the eighteenth century were forerunners
of the approaching end,—that " the grand catastrophe
of God's drama draws near, apace," and that, long before
the general judgment, Christ will appear on earth, a second
time, to work out his redeeming purposes. Accordingly,
when referring to the Messianic Judgment (not the general)
at the end of our present age, he says that in the midst of
the great revolution that will then occur, " Our Lord Jesus
will suddenly come down from heaven, and go himself
conquering and to conquer; for *what but the greatest
prejudice* can induce Christians to think that the coming
of our Lord, spoken of in so plain terms by the three
Evangelists, is the *last* coming before the universal and

* *Tyerman's Life of Fletcher*, 21.
† Ibid.

the end of the world,"* *i. e.,* the ultimate end or goal of all history.

In 1777, or twenty-two years after this, having devotedly studied the subject still more, he was yet of the same mind. In his " *Doctrines of Grace,* etc.," he says, " In the Psalms, Prophets, Acts, Epistles, and especially the Revelation, we have a variety of promises that, in the day of His displayed power, Christ will ˙come in His glory to judge among the Gentiles, wound the kings in the day of his wrath, root up the wicked, fill the places with their dead bodies, smite in sunder Antichrist and the heads over divers countries, and *lift up His own triumphant head, on this very earth, where he once bowed His wounded head, and gave up the ghost.'* Compare Psalm 110 with Acts 1. 11, 2 Thess. 1. 10, Rev. 19. 11, etc. In that Great Day, another dispensation shall take place. Then Allelujah! Then the marriage of the Lamb is come! The Lord God omnipotent reigneth! Then, ' Blessed and Holy is he who hath part in the First Resurrection.' ˙ Blessed are the meek, for they shall inherit the earth.' The thousand years, the times of refreshing, have come, the times of the restitution of all things. May the Lord hasten this Gospel Dispensation, and, till it take place, may *'the Spirit and the Bride say, Come.'*"†

In 1784, or twenty-nine years after his first letter, he openly repudiated in his " *Socinianism Unscriptural,*" the Unitarian or Socinian theory, even as he did Rome's theory, which still lingers in Protestant denominations, that we are in the millennium now, or that it will come by civilization, culture, and Church agencies before the Lord appears.

---

* *Tyerman's Life of Fletcher,* 21.   *Benson's Life of Fletcher,* 366.
† *Tyerman's Life of Fletcher,* 377.

After quoting Isa. 66. 15-24, he adds, "Here ends
Isaiah's account of that glorious reign of Jehovah Shiloh,
which the Fathers called the *'Millennium,'* as being to
last a thousand years, and during which it is probable our
Lord will use these extraordinary means to keep all the
Nations in the way of obedience : (1) A constant display
of His goodness over all the earth, but particularly in and
about Jerusalem where He will manifest His glory, and
bless His happy subjects with new manifestations of His
presence. (2) A distinguishing interposition of Providence
which will withhold Messiah's wonted blessings from the
disobedient. Zech. 14. 17. (3) The constant endeavors of
the Saints, Martyrs, Patriarchs, Prophets, and Apostles
raised from the dead, and conversing with such men as
Moses and Elijah did with our Lord's disciples upon the
Mount of Transfiguration. (4) The care that the Lord
will take to set apart for the ministry, under His glorified
saints, those who in every nation shall distinguish themselves by their virtue and their piety. Isa. 66. 20, 21.
(5) A standing display of the ministration of condemnation
as appears from Isa. 66. 24, and other parallel Scriptures.
(6) At the same time, an occasional display of the ministration of righteous mercy will work upon their hopes.
How will those hopes be fired when they shall see the
" Lamb of God " standing on Mount Sion, and with him the
one hundred and forty-four thousand worthies " having His
Father's name," Divine Majesty, Irrisistible Power, Ineffable
Love, and Bliss Inexpressible, " written on their foreheads."
Rev. 14. 1-5. But (7) what will peculiarly tend to keep
men from lapsing into rebellion against God, will be the
long life of the godly, and the untimely death of those who
shall offer to tread the paths of iniquity. The godly

shall attain to the years of antediluvian patriarchs, and the wicked shall not live out half their days. They shall not live above a hundred years; or, to speak after our manner, they shall die in their childhood. Isa. 66. 17-25.*

So spake this " Seraph," triumphant to his dying day in the unwavering faith of the " Primitive Church," and word of God, that there is no Millennium till the Lord comes! How sad that the Church should have departed so far, in our day, from this " precious faith."

XII.—COKE'S TESTIMONY.

The Rev. Thomas Coke, LL.D., Fellow of Jesus College, Oxford, England, was the first Methodist Bishop, ordained by John Wesley, Sept. 2, 1784, to cross the seas with two presbyters, in order to ordain *Rev. Francis Asbury* as joint Bishop with himself over the American Methodists, then numbering fifteen thousand members. Asbury was ordained in Baltimore, Md., Dec. 27. 1784, and thus the " Methodist Episcopal Church in the United States " was organized, and took rank as a separate denomination ;— "Wesley, the Chief Pastor," and " Father of the whole family ; "—" Coke, the Elder Brother ; "—Asbury, his " equal in the Sacred Office." Let us hear Coke's testimony as to the premillennial faith. We quote from his great Commentary :

" The *First Resurrection* is a particular one *preceding* the general one at least *a thousand years*. Blessed and holy in all senses of the word are they who are admitted to partake of this blessed state. On such the second death hath no power. The sons of the Resurrection, therefore,

---

shall not die again, but live in eternal bliss, as well as enjoy
all the glories of the Millennium; be priests of God
and Christ, and reign with Him a thousand years.
Nothing is more evident than that this prophecy of the
Millennium and of the First Resurrection has not yet been
fulfilled,—even though it were taken in a figurative sense.
*If Satan was bound in Constantine's time, when can he be
said to be loosed?—or how could the Saints and the Beast,
Christ and Antichrist, reign at the same time?* This
prophecy, therefore, remains yet to be fulfilled, even though
the Resurrection be taken allegorically, *which yet the text
cannot admit without the greatest torture and violence.*
The Death and Resurrection here mentioned must be
concluded to be real. If the martyrs rise only in a spiritual sense, then ' the rest of the dead ' rise only in a spiritual sense. But, if the ' rest of the dead ' really rise, the
martyrs rise in the same manner. There is no differ-
ence between them. And we should be cautious and
tender of making the ' First Resurrection ' an allegory,
lest others should reduce the Second into an allegory too,
like those Paul mentions, 2 Tim. 2. 17, 18. In general,
that there shall be such a happy period as the Millennium,
is the plain and express doctrine of Dan. 7. 27, Psalm
2. 8, Isa. 11. 9, Rom. 11. 25, and of all the prophets as well
as of St. John. And we daily pray for the accomplishment
of it, in saying, ' *Thy Kingdom come!*' But, of all the
prophets, John is the only one who has declared particularly, and in express terms, that *the martyrs shall rise to
partake of the felicities of this Kingdom, and that it shall
continue upon earth a thousand years.* In short, the doctrine of the Millennium was generally believed in the first
three and purest Ages, and this belief was one principal

cause of the fortitude of the *Primitive Christians.* They even coveted martyrdom in hope of being partakers of the privileges and glories of the martyrs in the First Resurrection. The doctrine lay depressed for many ages, but it sprang up again at the Reformation and will flourish together with the study of the Revelation."*

XIII.—BENGEL'S TESTIMONY.

" In 1716, Zeltner published a Dissertation on the Millennium, in which he expresses his surprise that anyone can shrink from the title of *'Chiliast,'*† because it is plain that he who receives the divine authority of the Apocalypse must also of necessity admit the Thousand Years, in some sense. Well said. But there are some who, compelled by this text, hold that there is to be a remarkable and long-continued tranquillity of the Church, and maintain this with impunity. But wherefore so? On this ground alone, viz., that *they remove from* THEIR *mouth the Thousand Years which have proceeded* FROM THE MOUTH OF GOD! It is of no advantage thus to alarm good men. *These* THOUSAND YEARS *do not run a single step simultaneously with the Times of the Beast, nor do they wholly* PRECEDE *them, but wholly* FOLLOW *them.* They violate this excellent system of prophecy who blend together the Times of the Beast and the Thousand Years. . . . In a short time they who believe that the Millennium is at hand will be found to have the privilege of the true meaning, rather than those who contend that it is past. Nor do they delay the course of the sun who speak against it. . . . *I*

---

* *Coke's Comm. N. T. II,* 1004, 1005. *New York,* 1812, *for the Methodist Connexion in U. S. A.*

† That is, One who believes in the " *Thousand Years.*"

had rather be regarded as a maintainer of the THOUSAND YEARS, *which Prophecy publishes so decidedly, than take part with the indiscriminate* ANTI-CHILIASTS *who, under this name of theirs, assail even the plain letter of Prophecy, and trample upon truth and error alike.* The mystery of God is in progress, and is finished when the Beast is destroyed and Satan is bound. That consummation approaches nearer and nearer. It comprises events by far the most important, and most closely connected with the glory of God. The knowledge of these events from day to day emerges into greater clearness, distinctness, and readiness of discernment. Meantime it is highly necessary to oppose the extreme rage of the Devil. But to speak against God, whose mystery it is, as many do ; to weaken the Oath of the Angel who confirms it ; ignorantly to assail interpreters who handle the subject in a befitting manner ; and, by thus assailing them, hunt after favor among those of like character with themselves ;—will not this, at last, be *hard* to the person himself ? Acts 9. 5. On the other hand, care must be taken not to attribute to the Millennium things which are reserved for Eternity itself." *

---

* *Gnomon N. T.*, *pp.* 1056, 7, *Lond.*, 1862. Bengel's *Double Millennium* was an error into which Wesley did not fall. But, as Dorner well says, " It served as a light toward the Truth." Remarkable are Bengel's works concerning the " *Beast.*" " The *Beast from the Sea* is the Papacy of Hildebrand, but the *Beast out of the Bottomless Pit* will have a quite new and singular character of wickedness, on account of which he is called the ' *Man of Sin.*' *Antichrist*, the *Man of Sin*, as being about to come in the *Nineteenth Century* (*Sæculo XIX*) could not be retarded by the Roman Power of the first and following centuries." *Gnomon N. T.*, on 2 *Thess.* 2. 3, *p.* 759, *Lond.*, 1862.

XIV.—THE WESLEY HYMNS.

From the official *"Hymnal"* of the American Methodist Episcopal Church, approved by the Board of Bishops, *Hunt & Eaton*, New York.   1877.

Hymn 924; a prayer for the fulness of the Gentiles, the Conversion of the Jews, and the Coming of the Lord.

> *" Come, Lord,"* Thy glorious Spirit cries,
>   And souls beneath the altar groan ;
> *" Come, Lord,"* the Bride on earth replies,
>   " And perfect all our souls in one."
>
> Pour out the promised gift on all ;
>   *Answer the universal " Come !"*
> *The fulness of the Gentiles call,*
>   *And take Thine ancient people home.*

Hymn 926; in which the work of both Advents is seen in one picture.

> *The glory of the Lord displayed*
>   Shall *all* mankind *together* view ;
> And what His mouth in truth hath said,
>   *His own almighty hand shall do.*

Hymn 946; looking for the Advent and Millennial Age.

> Our residue of days or hours,
>   Thine, wholly Thine, shall be ;
> And all our consecrated powers
>   A sacrifice to Thee,
>
> *Till Jesus in the clouds appear*
>   To saints on earth forgiven,
> *And bring the grand Sabbatic year,*
>   *The Jubilee of Heaven.*

Hymn 952 ; listening for the Bridegroom.

> Blest object of our faith and love,
>> *We listen for Thy welcome voice ;*
> Our persons and our works approve,
>> And bid us in Thy strength rejoice ;
> *Now let us hear the mighty cry,*
> *And shout to find the Bridegroom nigh.*

Hymn 954 ; ready to meet the Bridegroom.

> *He comes, He comes* to call
>> The nations to His bar,
> ⁻*And take to glory all*
>> *Who meet for glory are ;*
> Made *ready* for your full reward,
> *Go forth with joy to meet your Lord.*

Hymn 1013 ; the grand old Judgment Hymn

> *Lo ! He comes, with clouds descending,*
>> Once for favored sinners slain ;
> *Thousand thousand saints attending,*
>> Swell the triumph of his train :
>> *Hallelujah ! Hallelujah !*
> GOD APPEARS ON EARTH TO REIGN.

Hymn 1014 ; Christ's Epiphany in glory for the Rapture of His Saints.

> Sun and Moon are both confounded,
>> Darkered into endless night,
> *When, with Angel Hosts surrounded,*
>> *In His Father's glory bright,*
>>> *Beams the Saviour,*
> *Shines the everlasting Light.*

> *Lo! 'tis He! our hearts' desire,*
>   *Come for His espoused below ;*
> Come to join us with His choir,
>   Come to make our joys o'erflow ;
>   Palms of Victory,
> *Crowns of glory, to bestow!*

Hymn 1018; Christ's assumption of the sovereignty of the world, at the sounding of the Seventh Trumpet.

> *He comes ! He comes ! the Judge severe,*
> *The Seventh Trumpet speaks Him near ;*
> The lightnings flash, his thunders roll ;
> How welcome to the faithful soul !
>
> *Shout, all the people of the sky,*
> And *all the saints* of the Most High ;
> Our Lord who now His right obtains,
> *Forever and forever reigns.*

Hymn 1024; we shall be like Him; watching for His Appearing.

> O may we all be found
>   Obedient to Thy word,
> *Attentive to the trumpets' sound,*
>   *And looking for our Lord.*
>
> O may we thus insure
>   A lot among the blest ;
> And *watch* a *moment* to secure
>   An everlasting rest.

Hymn 650; the Hope of the Coming of Jesus from Heaven.

> Thou who hast kept us to this hour,
>   O keep us faithful to the end,
> *When, robed in majesty and power,*
>   *Our Jesus shall from Heaven descend,*

His friends and witnesses to own,
And seat us on His glorious throne !

Hymn 1030; the Hope of the Resurrection brought near, by faith.

O what a Blessed Hope is ours !
While here on earth we stay,
We more than taste the heavenly powers,
And antedate that day :
We feel the Resurrection near,
Our life in Christ concealed,
And with His glorious presence here
Our earthen vessels filled.

Hymn 1065; longing for Christ's Appearing.

Thou know'st in the spirit of prayer
We long Thy Appearing to see,
Resigned to the burden we bear,
But longing to triumph with Thee !

Hymn 1046; changed into the same image at " that day."

The heavenly treasure now we have
In a vile house of clay ;
But Christ will to the utmost save,
And keep us to " that day."

Him eye to eye we there shall see,
Our face like His shall shine ;
O what a glorious company,
When saints and angels join !

These thrilling strains are but specimens of many more, standing beside the Advent melodies from the souls of Denny, Milton, Cowper, Heber, Watts, Bathurst, Montgomery, Newton, Alford, and McCheyne.   No denomination on earth can boast a more copious or complete Hymnology in reference to the Coming of the Lord than the American Methodist Episcopal Church.   May the rafters be made to ring with them, throughout the length and breadth of the land, and every Camp Meeting be a Prayer and a Hallelujah to the Coming One !

THE SPIRIT OF WESLEY.

" Would to God that all party names, and unscriptural phrases and forms, which have divided the Christian world, were forgot, and that we might all agree to sit down together as humble, loving disciples at the feet of our common Master, to hear His word, to imbibe His Spirit, and to transcribe His life into our own " (*Preface to Wesley's Notes on the New Testament*).

Amen and Amen !

THE FUTURE AGE AND THE KINGDOM.

The Middle-Point, or Center of the " Last Things," in the O. T. Scriptures, is the *Parousia* of Christ, which, first of all, includes both Advents in one undiscriminated picture, and presents two ages : (1) the pre-Messianic before the Parousia ; (2) the Messianic, after the Parousia ; the one called "this world," or "age" (αἰὼν ὁ οὗτος), the other the " world," or "age to come " (αἰὼν ὁ μέλλων), and this " world to come," the " Future Age," is on the earth, not in heaven. It is the historical development of the Kingdom of God, which, under Messiah's administration, is called the Messianic Kingdom. Later O. T. prophecy separates the Advents into (1) a Parousia in humiliation, and (2) a Parousia in glory. In the first, Messiah comes as a Virgin-born Child, appears as riding on a colt, teaches, works miracles, suffers, dies, and rises again, ascending to heaven. In the second, Messiah comes from heaven, riding on the clouds, attended by his Angels, raises the righteous dead, destroys his enemies, restores Israel, and sets up his kingdom of glory on the earth, all nations obedient to his sway. The first coming was the hope of the Ancient, the second is the hope of the Christian Church. In later O. T. prophecy, the Messianic Age itself is subdivided into (1) "this present Age" or "World," and (2) the "Age or World to come." Here the Second Advent becomes the Middle-Point of the Future. New Testament prophecy resumes this later development of O. T. prophecy, and expands the whole Messianic Period, or Total Time of the Kingdom, into two Ends and three Ages : (1) our present Age, or present world followed by the Second Advent, and the Kingdom of the Thousand Years, or Millennial Age ; (2) the Millennial Age followed by the Last Judgment and Regenesis of the Planet and (3) the Eternal State, or Endless Age. In all these representations, Jerusalem, the Holy City, is ever present, in it various fortunes, whether of destruction or of glory, and never disappears from the picture. The early Christians understood this well, familiar with the prophets, and instructed by inspired Apostles who themselves had learned of Christ. It was reserved for John, in his Apocalypse, to unfold the Messianic Ages and Ends in their temporal order and succession, and open out, with distinct expression, the period of the Thousand Years and the two Resurrections and Judgments. This simple presentation of the development of prophecy lies at the root of all the language of the early Apologists of Christianity, and of the early Fathers of the Church. It explains the language of *Clement* and of *Justin*, as of all the rest, concerning the " *Future Age*," the " *Age to come*," and the " *Kingdom*," by which they meant the " Millennial Age." It was impossible for them not to regard our present Age as *premillennial*, and by necessity of the representation in both Testaments the Second Advent, which closes our present Age, could itself only be a *premillennial Advent*, the one glorious Hope of the Church. The Kingdom of the Thousand Years, consequently, could only be one phase in the great development of the Kingdom of God on earth. And this reconciles all the various ideas and expressions used in the Scriptures in reference to the " Kingdom." In its fulness, it is past, it is present, it is to come ; it is inward and spiritual existing now, it is outward and visible yet to exist ; it is heavenly ; it is a kingdom of grace ; it is a kingdom of glory ; it is earthly ; it is temporal ; it is everlasting. In its *forms* it is many, in its *essence* it is one. It has various dispensations. It is above, it is below, and its highest consummation is the realization of the Will of God on earth as it now is realized in heaven ; a consummation begun now, developed in the Age to come, and completed in the Eternal State. We cannot wonder, therefore, at the ardor of the early Christians in their hope of the Advent, the Resurrection of the righteous, the coming Kingdom and the Glory, and on this very earth. It thrilled their souls. It led them to martyrdom. It was a premillennial Church that overthrew paganism and the Roman Empire, and won victories in lands where Cæsar's eagles never flew. It was missionary to the core. It never begged for money. It laid its offering of body and soul, a living, yet bleeding and loving sacrifice, upon the altar of God. It had a priestly heart, like Jesus. It looked to the glory to be revealed. In the beautiful words of Neander, that greatest of Church historians, "It was a solace and support to the Christians to anticipate that even here, on earth, the scene of their sufferings, the Church was destined to triumph in its perfected and glorified state. They framed a spiritual idea of the happiness of this period (the millennial age) perfectly corresponding with the essence of the Gospel, conceiving under it nothing else than the dominion of the Divine Will, the undisturbed and blissful reunion of the whole community of saints, and the restoration of harmony between a sanctified humanity, and all nature transfigured to its primitive innocence" (*Hist. Chr. Rel. I*, 650). Let us not forget the important testimony already quoted. "This precious hope," says Dr. Schaff, "through the whole Age of Persecution, was a copious fountain of encouragement and comfort under the pains of that martyrdom which sowed in blood the seed of a glorious harvest for the Church" (*Hist. Chr. Chh. I*, 299). Nor was there a dissentient voice among the Apostolic Fathers who stood nearest to the Apostles themselves. "All," says Dorner, "were at one; men of the Johannine school, like Polycarp and Papias; of the Pauline, like Ignatius and Clement of Rome; of the Petrine, like Barnabas; of that of James, like Hermas and Hegesippus" (*Person of Christ I*, 143). In the words of Alford "The whole Church, for three hundred years, understood Rev. 20. 1–6 in a plain literal sense," and "it is the most cogent instance of unanimity which primitive antiquity presents" (*N. T. II, part 2*, 1088). To "revive, enforce, and defend" this doctrine of the "Primitive Church," with the rest, Wesley was raised up of God. Has the temporal prosperity and wealth of his followers served to banish it from their faith and their love? Other denominations are rekindling their torches with this "precious hope." Shall the Methodist Church slumber in the rear, or flame in the van? Worldly prosperity quenched this "blessed hope" to make room for the Papacy with its carnal caricature of the Kingdom before the time! Do we yet love Rome so well as to cover ourselves with her rags, or, like Wesley, shall we too, "*revive, enforce, and defend the Primitive Faith?*" Wesley lived before the *French Revolution* at the close of the last century. Had he lived to share the views of the great expounders of prophecy, held as a result of the outburst of Infidelism all over Europe then, and the waves of which are upon us to-day, how his pen would have sketched the coming *Infidel Antichrist*, as well as the "Antichrist at Rome!" How he would have pointed to the coming of Christ as the only "Hope" of the Church!

"I HAVE lost my friend Wesley, but I shall see him again, perhaps soon, even upon earth where the sufferers for Christ are to rise and reign in His spiritual kingdom, for a Thousand Years" (*Walter Churchey, Esq., the friend of Coke, Fletcher, and Cowper. Tyerman III,* 579).

www.ingramcontent.com/pod-product-compliance
Lightning Source LLC
Chambersburg PA
CBHW020526030426
42337CB00011B/560